Philomena,
Thanks for Listening
+ Believing!
Feel The Bern!
Mike J
5/16

smitten by harpies

mike jurkovic

smitten by harpies

©-Copyright-Mike Jurkovic-2015

All images - Mike Jurkovic

First edition published 2016

Streets I Have Known, or an Introduction to Mike Jurkovic

I was commuting to the Hudson Valley from Albany once a month back in the early '90s, hosting an open mic, and Mike heard about it somewhere along the way, in those pre-Internet days when readings were advertised via flyers, or listings in the local newspaper or even, unimaginably, by word of mouth. He was not so forward as to call, so he sent me a postcard care of the A.I.R. Studio. It was addressed to "Miss Rice," a title he has since learned I gave up at the age of reasoning, around ten or so, but the passion about his poetry was evident. "I'm very interested in reading in Kingston or Albany or wherever." He came to my reading, and to many readings after. I was one of the gang that populated his *Voices of the Valley* reading series that followed, after my return full-time to the land of apples and Huguenots. He came to my various experiments too, and soon we became family, through the blood of arts.

His poems have moved over the years to expand beyond the provincial territory of his own backyard (an interesting enough place) to include the folktales and legends of his green imagination. His language combines nouns and adjectives in unlikely, startling ways. Think of a Catskill yarn-spinner in blue jeans, tie-dyed tuxedo and Nike'd feet, swinging in the hammock of what's left of the yawping counterculture our neck of the U.S. woods was once famous for. From coal towns to museums of self–pleasure, short blue skirts to the soothsayers of Zuccotti, he bears bold witness to our times, to a degree one might expect of the poets of half a century before him. Think straight Ginsberg, urban Snyder, moderately expanded Kerouac and you'll begin to sense what his poetry is like. Add a dash of romance, working man's malaise, Crowley's sage fool just short of epic stumble off the tarot's cliff, and you will get closer.

But read the poems for yourself. Settle into a cozy throne of rattan, turn down the Coltrane to a haze of soulful mist, pour yourself a shot of Grey Goose, and turn the pages. You will find a comrade, a patriot (in the most accurate, global definition of the word) a crusader and, especially, a brother traveler on these mean streets of Earth that we all pass over.

- Cheryl A. Rice
February, 2016

for Emily, always

and thanks to Calling All Poets for keeping me honest

Table of Contents

Runner-up
(a) Trophy Prose
High Diver
The Nicest Creations
Weak Cappuccino
Red Knots
California's Newest Medicinal
Quality Control Guy
Hebetude
I Shot the Sheriff
If I Should Die
this vast engine
Broadly Phonetic
Crippled Witness
Sunny Lots
Gravity Gets Us All
Something about the hallway
Half Shitty Days
Our Holy Songs
Clearing House
Pale Diaspora
One Body
Roswell
Her Finery
The Gnomist
Mongrel
Sacrament
a history of feminist driving
All the Lawns are Perfect
wrinkled, blue
The Blonde w/Blue Shoes
Her trio nimble
Wounded Cassandra
Hitler's Florist
Color Code
Maggie's Piano
Pacific Trash Vortex

Two Wives Ago

It's a beautiful thing. Stockpiled.
Vacuum sealed. Purchased a little each pay day
for the last fifteen years
and two wives ago. Neither could see
my reasoning so I gave up trying.
You can only save yourself in the end.
Everyone else drains your supplies.

Dated. Rotated. Each 50mm can
checked monthly for corrosion.
In this room mostly corn meal
and 50lb bags of sugar.
A tunnel to the highway
shelved floor to ceiling
w/corn and tuna.

In this room alone, my water.

Two Doors Down

There is no corner house for your latest desire but there is
a cozy duplex, just off Main, behind the shoe repair and
water department. Two doors down there's a cute artisanal
bakery where cupcakes become dreams and a toothless
man rails for mince. The Dutch Apple Chocolate is
sometimes dry. Other than that it's a quiet town, sunny and
white, where Kalashnikovs make wealth and Lotto governs
the poor. The ringleader lights his flaming hoops as lost
girls play hopscotch w/religion in their ear buds. The way
is cleared for the prophet. The riser erected. The carpet
tacked down. The faithful stampede. Bring their kids to the
show. Tomorrow could be the be all and end all but it's still
just a staircase, a footnote. A cheap sleight of hand
God sometimes uses then overdubs strings. Then on
Wednesday the town board votes and on Thursday
another mass shooting.

w/Will Nixon

Screaming Jay Hawkins and Me in Our Prime

I'm lost in a parking lot on the left coast
w/an Afghan Kush and Grey Goose buzz
when Screamin' Jay Hawkins
jumps the Sierras screaming:
"What can I do w/eighty-six kids
'n each momma wantin' my jam?!"
"Get in motherfucker!" I salvo,
kicking the gas like a mule bucks gravity.

Hurtling down coastal route one
w/an oft-subpoenaed legend in my car doesn't faze me.
Hell no! I expect these things from time to time,
the brain unhinged, the whole world gone batshit.
Screamin' Jay riffing in the passenger seat is no more nuts
to me than dumping poisons in the ocean to my left.
Its vast sky full w/the moans of our daughters'
womb engines, pumping out pilots, privates, and warlords
no one believes can win anymore.

the haloes in her glasses

Trish MaClaver
had a sinister tic.
A lithium logic
that begged dedication.
Her mercy flew in fragments
and she made a darker jazz
w/a set degree of fixture
and no sliding scale,
that dates back to seventh grade
when I stole my first kiss.

The sun was bright that day.
The air unseasonably clean.
The Christmas lights haloed
in her glasses. I couldn't resist.
I took her right there. Mouth to mouth.
Miss Norton flustered. We were two of a kind.
Desire an un-tempered skill.

Prone to the mad calls of profit
our hearts locked perfectly. And all through college
we plotted our motive. Sold pot to raise funds.
Took our first shipment of Armalite Colts
and a box of Berettas. Then we read,
in the Armed Tribune, about a new arms maker:
Glock. It was '63: The Beatles on the BBC.
I saw here standing there w/haloes in her glasses
and proposed.

We invested heavy. Under the table.
Across the boards. Across the Da Krong River
w/freedom in the hull. Then she miscarried
and we took a break. Sailed Greece. Made connections.
Made some calls and flew to Taiwan. Nairobi.
We never talked of kids again.

We went low profile in the eighties
but it didn't last long. We were one of a kind
so we went to Detroit. Camdem. Memphis. Newburgh.
Selling cheap and plentiful to both sides. Cops. Robbers.
Makes no diff. Everyone's gearing up for survival.

War unabated. Abroad. At home. To avoid bloodshed
we vacationed on private islands. Even after retiring,
we got involved deep w/the Middle East. Fattening kings,
killing their house. That income set us up to this,
our friends and family all in one room,
bearing a torch to her grave.

Neighbor of Alleged Bomber

I'm just the neighbor
on the night shift really.
I barely knew the guy or why
he'd blow up Main Street.
But I suspect he was
a quiet man who had reached his limit.
A quiet man who heard too loudly
the lie of the industrialists.
A regular guy
w/a short fuse
like the rest of us. Tense. Occluded.
Huddling by the Blu-Ray,
hoping *NCI* or a real time bombing can distract us.
But nothing does. The soldiers go door to door
till they crash through yours and your gun is in
the other room where your children used to be.

Ballad of Cigarette Monty (*rw*)

There you go naked again
banging your head on the rafters
supporting the sky. Knocking the birds
loose from their nesting flights.

Your thoughts are spinning
in untoward directions.
Your brain has lost its moorings,
your Cadillac pills aren't working.

On the far side of the moon
you find Hoffa. There's a parade
but it drifts like lilies in Heaven.
The moon never knows where to land
when the lovelorn await momentum.

There're cameras in your garden
and microphones in the bath.
There is no escape
from the compound of needs.
Only hurried exits, brief returns,
the jinni obscuring our dreams.

w/Will Nixon

My Fifth Minute

In case you missed it,
my mullet days are over.
For whose Divine kinship
accords a haircut and a fish
the same paradigm?

What Creation theory fathoms
this follicle fashion and bequeaths
this bottom feeder the crown
of the last five decades?

I have my suspicions
but now is not the time.
They play by the rules
at this open mic and my fifth minute
crawls close. Besides,

No one wants to hear my shit.
Not now. Not ever, and especially
when circling the snack tray
for grapes and stale crackers.

10th 'n Brutal

she was
last seen
in a
recyke dumpster
behind a market
on 10th 'n Brutal
known for its meats,
customer service,
and locksmiths.

all the world's
casual horror
rents on
10th 'n Brutal.
a graphic novel
dungeon town
where the common beg
and flagellate.

the mayor's last penny
bought alibis
on 10th 'n Brutal
where nostalgia makes
the dick hard.
where she was
last seen
in a recycke dumpster,
her ring finger
nowhere
to be
found

loodle

We'd progressed to the point
of extinction. So per her suggestion
I fuck myself and grab an' espresso.
Children of the pestilence
say the darnedest things.

East 138

Through our debris
Our children walk
Barefoot in barrios
Burdened at birth,

Cry the cold china
Billboards in Harlem
East 138
I still call you home.

Turn back the promise
The premise, the menace
East 138
I still call you home.

Abandoned like babies
Burnt and begotten
Over a river of peril
Standing alone,

At the crossroads, a beggar
Of jade and Jehovah
Hustlin' for handouts
From shadows long stilled,

Spit out the devil
The demon, the donor,
The monster, the baby
The shrill of the dead,

Run the cold plasma
Over hordes of the faithful
East 138
I still call you home.

The Great Movie Begins

As I take my cushion,
The great movie begins
Just as I have jumped
An LA freeway divider
To penetrate
the voluptuous young thing
eager to please.
When the aliens,
Prizing my secretions
More than she
Radiate into the room:
Big black eyes
On shark fin heads
Their hydra like fingers
Snake towards me
As the music swells
And I jump from her allure.
Out a window
Down a blind alley
With the voice of the kingfish calling
'Save The Secret! Save The Secret!"
I carjack a Nimbus
And levitate over
The streets of San Fran,
Morphing to Manhattan
Where the terrorists,
In league with our government
Have taken the U.N. hostage

An' I'm cocked 'n loaded n'
Special effected to the gills, baby
As one by one
I pluck 'em off:
My president,
Then Ali-Komma Komma
And his henchmen.
The Secretary of Defense
The alien horde.
The Interior Minister
Almost escapes
But I taser him
As the starlet, still wet,
takes me in.
The bell rings:
My meditation over.

something clicks

and invariably
I break from
your savagery
in favor of my own

Double Light

It's 6:30 and the moon's
upside down
And I palpate
at the thought of blood.
Arming myself
for a rush hour rip
through downtown
where you'll watch 'em fall
in my wake.

I knew this day was coming
'n now here it is. So I set about
calmly, slowly. The morning news
low in the background
'cos no one gives a shit
until the bullets fly. Hit a child.
Hit your mother. We all fall when pierced
by double light.

irony

I needed to start a fire
so I bought my own book
back for a buck and
skinned a small animal
for dinner.

Weak Reeds

Sometimes it all seems so
prolonged. Protracted. Extended
beyond its natural life.
Sometimes the situations are so forced
you resent the abuse. The push 'n pull.
The shove 'n shank.
Sometimes all you hear is the clock
and the fridge making ice. Maybe a dying nightlight
exposes a clue. Maybe, if you just surrendered your
checkbook, it would all go away.

Our Town

There were no birds
and thus no sound but
the working of men
against themselves.
The wails of women
violated. The prayer of lambs
doused w/gas.

There were no birds
and thus the sky was black.
Bruised. The stars in hiding.
The sun in retreat. The moon
a pale frustration.

Dinner at Spillane's

The Order of the Gray Mustache
gathers at table four,
Where we meet each month
to toast Aleve and the head achieved
by mixing weed 'n oxy.

Everyone's had a cancer scare
and needs glasses. Has a parent
showing signs or is planning
a trip to France.

Our ladies grace the room.
We leverage for fine wine.
Tamp down our hyperbole.
Take a pill, from time to time,
to tighten a muscle
or lighten the load.

We binge watch
and talk of the dead.
Hold each other
in the dark,
hoping the meds
bring the morn.

she whispered me tales

She's a homegrown harpie
from another book of mine
you didn't read. Dusty Relix,
the rector's wife, who's down a quart
and making the truth sound easy.

Whispering me tales
of my own slapdash gene
and fetish twitch. The curious witherings
of the family root. Cousin Barney's penchant
for riding short trains. Aunt Sally's viral night.
Joey's odd tooth. Millie's deviant frescos.

But I'm biased, really. They're all I've got
and tall tales don't riff like they used to.
Time moving like winter will do that
to the eccentric soul. But she's on a roll
and I like her voice. Droll. Lilting,
giving the night a breath of joy.

4,000

I was in a wild barbarian area
doing happiness research,
When a storm surge rose the dead.
4,000 coffins uprooted, evicted,
adrift on the crushing tide.

Marking the animal calendar
stroke by stroke,
The dead flotilla surrendered:
Name, rank, serial number
Rounded smooth. Disappeared.

Skeletons intervene like shadows
on a godless moon
Where the entire tribe has fallen,
wasted on stolen blood.
Awaiting the flood, the fire,
to bury it all again.

Legend Holds

What the ladies said about Billy the Kid
was true: He hid under petticoats often
after coaxing the red dog sun from their loins. He'd rest in
the Sierra Blanca,
reading dime store novels
w/a grin that frayed at the edges.

His dusty boots, his crooked hats
cast shadows on the noose. Until one day
when some great love, or its proximity,
divided his bones for sport

w/Raphael Kosek & Will Nixon

My Inner Mexican

My inner Mexican
loves yard work.
The 20-horse growl of 8am,
the edger's obdurate cut.

We all look alike. Pushing seed,
laying turf. Watching your daughters
ready for class while tearing up
your flowers.

My inner Mexican
lives by the knife.
Ruts jalapeño. Sings tejano
in the night.

Adrift

Adrift (a-drift): adjective and adverb
In a drifting state-   drifting   un
certitude - incertitude   and doubt.
    Doubtfulness and dubiousness –
            a hes -1 — tation - - - suspense,
        Per - plexity or an embarrassment, A Dilemma,
            BeWiLDerMenT - a puzzle, a quandary,
                    timidity etc,   etcetc and
            FEAR!
Vacillation...Wav
                                        ering
in termination,   Vague   Hazy   FOGGY
    an obscure ambiguousness. An OpeN ?. A blind
bargain.   A PIG IN THE POKE and a LEAP In tHe darK.
        a fallibility we all
        feel, an   un-
        Reliability we all
        un -   TRUST.
        Apre-cariousness.
        I hesitate when
        I'm ADRIFT.. .. I
        flounder.... I miss
        my way.. . .1
        Wander
        AIMIessLy;
I beat about
        I lose myself I lose my HEAD and I PerPlex Those
    Around ME and
        I POSE , I PUzZlE and confUse, conFOUND,,
    BewilDEr and I doubT
        ETC.
                        ETC.
I'm uncertain, unsure, casual, ranDOm   and aimless, doubtful,
    dubious,
INSECURE and Un - stable. I'm InDeCiSIVE for sure and ir-

resolute and
unsettled,

      undecided, undetermined and ?able; experimental and
TENTATIVEly

              tentative.
      I'm vague. Indefinite. Ambiguous.
Equivocal.
Undefined, confused, in mysterious, cryptic
and veiled obscurity.
Undefinable!_   ORACULAR!!
Perplexing!

      Enigmatic AND pArAdOxIcAl, Apocryphal and
      Problematic
Cantankerous!   FalliblE,   questionaBLE - - -
debatable- - -

      UNTrusTWorthY

                   unrel
iable.   and   ir-responsible
SO, don't deal with me when I'm
puzzled,   pickled,   perPlexed
OR I'm lost ADRIFT at sea, ai fault
at

      loss of I'm at my wit's end.........distracted...........and
distraught.................. A   D   R   I   F   T...

Yearbook

Frost's granddaughter convinced me of my brilliance
as she held me between her legs
like I was the last poet on earth.

We were young so sex closed the deal.
Rock the girl and you were
the next big thing in the land of *lettres*,
bite her neck and she read your words with worship.

Hell, I could do that. It was
sophomore year after all and I had
plenty of testosterone. Discovering
tongue along cleavage, lips upon belly,
tracing the sweat down her spine.

I had a way with alliteration
that was wholly American, she said.
My hands on her feverish ass
as I foraged for her fulcrum -
breathing warm along her panty line,
the color that of open sky

Blitzkrieg Alphabet

In that bright shiny moment
before the abyss, before Buddha reposed
like the hovering hawk, the mermaids sang
high in the harbor. The foghorn blew uncivil shanties.
The tides had forgotten. The language we had
was tiny. So tiny that faith was a
blitzkrieg alphabet recruiting the clown
and his Stage Right Singers
to ignore the rain. Ignore the nurses
adjusting the lights
and stare into
the dark, blank plate
where the will of the main frame
is sworn daily.

w/Will Nixon

The Old Shithouse

By the light of my own effigy
I set out from the village
Seeking wider lanes

An emotional gnome
Cutting loose
The vines

Of garbage truck tyranny,
The traffic
And turbulence

It seeks to induce.
Primarily on
The nervous system

Of lights and signs
Tolls
And truant officers

Joyriding
On the
County's dime.

Normally
I wouldn't mind
But today is today
And how many tomorrows
is anyone's guess.

So I took it
upon myself
figuring no one else
would bother

Lest I paid them
or promised
a virgin.

So without coin
or virginity
I set out

w/o looking back.
A mistake I'd made
once too often

and left
the old shithouse
behind.

It Was a Nice Day

You never walk New York
the same way twice
and that's a great relief
for this clan of criminal lovers
whose teeth don't match.
Whose peevish complaints
annoy me.
Leave me
unattended.

I only blew up the building
because I could. It was a nice day.

I only blew up the building
because my back was up
against the wall
and I needed recreation.
Because I wanted to,
I had to. Because the line
between gang
and government
is gone

Deathbed

The acid was prime he'd beam,
brothel bound during MK-Ultra.
But it backfired he'd boast.
His jaw slack, his eyes accepting
the last Bronx light. *I didn't fall
to the mind control and followed the Dead
instead.*

Jerry's leads were elliptical he'd burn
and begin again. *After the acid swept the shit away
I saw the futility of fighting each other.
So I swore upon that value
and lie here unafraid.*

above Colorado

My meds weave a trail
back to Pickle Back Hill
where my dreams have gotten
so strange and habitual I fear
we're all prone
to their odd tectonics.

I'm auctioning gifts
from the unfriended.
An unclean class
which had my doubts
all along.

But that's not the point
right now. Right now
five bucks gets ya
a Pan Am ashtray
from Flight 369
that last was seen
right before Roswell
in that azure space
above Colorado.

Where the sit-com substance
of bipolar kin
are betting on brain scans
and the bidding is slow.

salt water taffy

roll up your tents
dust off your boots
freaks, never scrutinize

stick out your tongue
extinguish the pool
the sacristy's on fire

take off your pants
finger your chin
the FBI is looking

she swore she saw
Murray the K
take off, with her boyfriend's wallet

trim the frost
from your beard
the Bronx will always glimmer

watch as Van Gogh
in the batters' cage
sings Spanish to a squirrel

w/Will Nixon

My Sister

In the umbra of banks
beneath humid stars
she serves a tumorous magic.

Labors in sour purpose.
Gives birth to good soldiers
like good girls do.

Lives in a country
I'll soon discard.

Tell Them, My Love

If they ask, my dear
tell them I died behind the wheel
waiting for the light to turn,

Waiting for the ass ahead of me
to discover his left foot from his right.

Tell them, my love, I died simpering
while the road crew widened thoroughfares,
smoothed the finish of my blackened heart.

Tell them, my love, should any be inclined to query
of my well-being, that I'm buried with the odometer,
the universal gear.

Tell them I withered in the heat.
The stewing froth of motion and mediocrity,
Prey to the rush and clatter,
the zooming zoom zoom of death.

Tell them, my love, I died in love.
With you, with them,
despite the miles between us

wishing I was home.

There Was a Fire Truck

There was a fire truck in the yard
and a screaming in the distance.

I had just polished the driver's side
when the phone rang and a fossil fear
froze me.

I was the new kid and not good w/maps.
So I let it ring. The screaming stopped.
Spit-shined the other side.

Mood Ring

On the night of my living friends
I improvise survival. Hold onto my hat.
For all I can barter
is small change and chatter.

So it looks like I'm fucked
when the ozone inverts
next Tuesday. So I'll stick
to the Stoli and Xanax
and wait for the speeches
to start.

Couldn't I

Did I have to pick
such a crowded field
to play in?

Couldn't I have been
a luthier or smithy,
a craft of hands
not language?

Couldn't I just build things?
Standing solid
instead of this cinerary
landscape of ideas,
wreaking the array
of orchids asunder.

Wallowing in affect,
couldn't I have plumbed
one board against another,

A bed, a chair,
what the village needs
Instead of my petitions
nailed to the wall

Guest List

By the time she escaped
The labyrinth of rooms,
The East Coast Apostasy
Had recast the guest list.
Dressed the hall,
Cut the lime.

Airbrush any mention
Of opium in the national trance:
Hank Williams and General George.
Franklin, Ben. Cobain, Kurt.
The 1890 Opium Tax.

I'm in the bar behind the learning curve
When two gray socialists
Pull up stools in Jimmy's Corner,
Where the least likeliest looking baritone
Solos for the red head
Just off the boat
In the shortest skirt
This side of Heaven,

Where I'll spend my days
Just fine, thank you.

Runner-up

The black smoke rising
sealed my fate.
I would not be
the dean of letters.

So, like every damaged American,
I shot my way through
the crowded mall –
The weapon like Helen
in my hands.

I drop the last large magazine,
a pistol takes my breath away.

(a) Trophy Prose

The winning collection
wasn't mine.
So my present state
is a tad unshaven.

Their rejection
concurred.
We went to great lengths
to find equilibrium

and here it is!
Telluric. Dogged by
doggerel. I can't make
heads or tails

of the trophy prose.
The Ringtone Asylum Award?
Big fuckin' deal.
I've got two

in a box
in the attic.
Kinda dusty,
as you might expect.

There's a sister
publication
that gives handjobs
and that prize

is
in
there
too.

High Diver

I'm an asshole!

I mean I'm really an asshole!

'Cos after hastily rolling
my last joint 'n
putting it in my pocket

I jump in the pool.

The Nicest Creations

like barium 'n mayo
my poems leave
a funky taste. Cut 'n run.
Lope along.

I prod them sometimes
this way or that.
But not often enough,
it seems.

They're not the nicest creations
but they're cut from the national darkness
and that proves something's wrong.
Life is amiss. Love is unclear.
A lot of us like that today.

Weak Cappuccino

The clouds were impressionistic
the day the Binary Men
condemned the river
and the consequent flood cleaned out
all the gullies and gutters. Swept away
hippie guitars and ganja.

In the square, the cook and the tour guide,
gone of adjective, tried to bully Genevieve
but she never cottoned to Neanderthals.
and no longer subscribed
to the astral divide. To her, Jesus made
weak cappuccino.

"I chronicle the inevitable," I said
as we set up shop above the waterline.
"I barter hope," she countered, unfolding a small table
and a new pack of cards.

As the water rose, the outcasts
stood in line. I took their cash.
She played the game. We made a mint.
The moon never caved.

Two steps ahead of the forthcoming climate,
our coffers were full. But I could never truly
get under her skin. Into her heart. I tried but
she was not your classic sestina or villanelle.
She was a ballad, a canto, a carol, a dirge.
A slow rolling blues that shed all distraction.

We fucked once but it was a business matter.
Still, I never did forget it: Like a wind shear,
we came at each other and came. Cut 'n dry.
The volcano exhausted.

"We had a good run," she said in departure.
"Thanks for the ride." The moon, sans despair.

w/Will Nixon

Red Knots

The rufa red knots, North America's most common
subspecies, flies the equivalent of the moon and back
in its lifetime. Now it faces extinction as we over-harvest
horseshoe crabs for the terminally corpulent.

Tell me again how we're not to blame
for everything dying on this planet.
Please, it wasn't clear the first time.

California's Newest Medicinal Marijuana Quality Control Guy

"It has a dry, dirt snipe personality
With a buzz that doesn't really buzz.
In the cud above the cerebellum
Like a rain cloud that won't rain.

Reminds me of the Mexican
We smoked before math,
The college Colombian, forty an ounce
Four joints got you high.

This hash a stronger stock I'd say.
In from Eureka along Willow Creek
A cultured growth gathered
at peak tonic and time.

I applaud this kush of Afghan cloning.
Its mild mayhem making me
King of my profession

Taste tester at minimum wage!

I don't need the bennies,
It's medicinal, right?

And if the union asks
I'll just say no.

Can I start tomorrow?"

Hebetude

Your hairline gives you away!
You're the dude I trashed
in the finals at Didscordia.

I knew perfection was elusive
even back then. But you? No.
You were your mother's son
pitching the party line.

"We're all privvy to beauty"
I think you said but
what do you say now w/a
twenty-four hour news cycle
littered w/crazies gouging, stabbing,
shooting each other? Each one a star
and best selling author
w/a smile as sleazy
as they come.

I Shot the Sheriff

Hard to tell
by this corrugate face
that I once wowed widows
from their panties and purse.

Until, like that Bob Marley song
that Clapton demolished,
I was cornered in San Bernardino
and shot the sheriff
from Sentinel Peak.
Slid deep into the carney.
Lathered up the bearded lady
every Tuesday when she shaved.

If I Should Die

What is history if not a fable agreed upon. – Napoleon

If I should die
before finishing this poem
Will you dovetail our voices
into one?

If I should die
before I conclude,
Please keep the truth
we carried into the war
that threatens to silence
the words we use
to shorten the distance between us.

this vast engine

w/a titular glance
the pale, one-armed daughter
turns me into sand.

She sidesteps cracks on Houston
w/a pill-shaped confidence.
She walks w/o ringtone
torching every black acre

Broadly Phonetic

These are tense times I know
but I'm not very keen
sharing this bunker
w/a mime. I'm gonna need
a much noisier bunk mate
to drown my head.

A mime makes a good neighbor:
Subdued, hushed. Sequestered w/a deaf ballerina
whose kids are all grown
w/careers more important
than Christmas.

Mimes can mean anything
unless you speak mime. And I don't.
I never believed in a second language,
lest they be the words of war. Deliberate, exultant.
Delivered by men in suits of each tongue.

That's the lingo we all capisce
and why I'm pleading my case
for another stateless archer
like myself: Forlorn, infirm.
Fearful. Like myself: Trying to outwit
the remaining hours.

Crippled Witness

The last of the wild blue mares has died
marking the fifteenth extinction this week.
But who's counting? The water's rancid.
The earth bears no fruit. The company bred
lack distinction. We feed them our children
for oil and water. Cancer and cures.
We lick their hull. Buff their urns.
Fuck between their soiled sheets.

Sunny Lots

I've grown older
and wary of the sales pitch.
The Doctrine. The old time TV
selling catheters and long term care,
cardiac stabilizers and sunny lots.
C Factors and urine flow and
vaginas that leak when you laugh.
Some little tumor they have
 a pill for. A potion for.
Proportioned individually
seven days a week. Helps hearing
but not hair growth. And, in the rare case
of a four hour erection, you could possibly
lose your mind.

Gravity Gets Us All

Turning back the mileage
Is no easy task
Once the lines and crow's feet
Impede upon the mask

The doctor's cut, the doctor's stitch
They make museum pieces
No matter how much you iron, babe
You're bound to see the creases

Gravity Gets Us All Baby
Gravity Gets Us All

Tummy in, shoulders back
Baggy shirts to hide the slack
Couch zucchini garden moans
A tad of rheumy in your bones

Face lifts and breast transplants
All to help a bad romance
Bags of sagging cellulite
Skin now hangs that once was tight

Gravity Gets Us All Baby
Gravity Gets Us All

So we pay for Botox daze
Two shots of Minoxidil
Yes we must live on and on
Just let the clocks stand still

The doctor's cut, the doctor's stitch
They make museum pieces
No matter how much you iron, babe
You're bound to see the creases

Gravity Gets Us All Baby
Gravity Gets Us All

Something about the hallway

Something about the hallway annoyed him. Or maybe it
was the time in the kitchen as he watched in horror, a child.
Penned in by Mom. Pen-knifed by Dad.

His sister said he had no talent
and the pressure in his head kept their contact at a
minimum. Which suited her fine
since most of the time she modeled for pulp magazines, and
kept company w/unpublished poets. His poetic career
began from imbalance. She was most comfortable posing
long hours for private detectives. His collection of clocks
stressed her out. Either way the floor cringed from the
weight of man and woman.

w/Marina Mati

Half Shitty Days

So you see there's good days and
Bad days and half shitty days
Which, I believe,
Most of us will testify to having
More often than not.

Half shitty days really have no point
of start or departure. Maybe you wake up
feeling grand but soon burn the toast
or step in cat pee.
Maybe a car hits a skunk
just in front of your house.
Perhaps you drop the soap in the shower
And whack your head on the towel bar.

Maybe the ride to work smoothes things out
but the job sucks. Then what?
Eight hours of suck?
Sounds like a good porno
But really, who can last that long?

Okay so lunch breaks the monotony
And jazz blows blue on NPR
But soon you drop a hammer on your foot
Or the fly in the ointment
Drowns in your coffee
And it's a shitty day again.

And just like that you're caught in the traffic home,
No one uses their signals
So you almost rear-end the guy
in front of you. That anxiety wears off
when, from out of nowhere
comes a kid in his daddy's Acura
cutting you off! Flipping the finger
as he heads off to produce
another illegitimate that you know
will someday pick your pocket
somewhere else in time.

But up ahead is home and all is well.
You hope. Who knows? Maybe your
Better half's had a whole bad day and
When compared to your half shitty one
well. . .who knows? Maybe they've had
a good day and that sunshine will make
your half shitty day really a quarter of a shitty day.
Who knows?

Who knows when half shitty days
become one or the other. Good or bad.
Who knows? Maybe that's the chore of being.

Our Holy Songs

Hustlers of the meaningless sky
turn rapture into milquetoast.
Swindle scripture. Plagiarize Debussy.
Fill the air w/patchouli.

These sharks dress like reverends.
Cauterize the flock.
Parcel out slander. Perjure their wives.
Bargain the grand equation.

These cons have no memory of Hendrix
So they corner the market
on all sharp objects.

Hustlers of the submarine
come in low at dawn.
Sell lifeboats that leak
in plain brown wrappers.

These rooks maintain their innocence.
Leaven their wallets w/bankrupt claret.
Balloon thieves puncture dogma.
Shower w/confetti. Write books about the Seine.
Substitute rubber bullets
w/armor piercing coin.
Smother the golden suffix,
burn guitars, our holy songs.

w/Will Nixon

Clearing House

I never could find a good use
for acoustic shadows so I'm
putting it right here next
to northing west. After twelve years of transfer
from notebook to napkin to notebook
a comic dance of retrofit has found its charnel ground.

Vague pronouncements is another orphan
successfully placed and please
Welcome to the page the noir flicker
where my head used to be.

Have you heard the one about
the clock doctor who stops me in the street
thirty-eight years to the day of his first house call,
To tell me how he cured the chimes in my father's
grandfather clock by removing my porn
from the pendulum's arc?

No, probably not because I just made it up. I do that
from time to time with wild corpuscle abandon.
Because having been such previously
my personality shards are all smoothed over.
No edge. No glare. No backstage help
through the bankrupt sprawl where a capsized blonde
places her bets in the dead, dry dust of Juarez.

Pale Diaspora

I'm sorry I mistook the Mercedes Benz logo for a peace
sign but I haven't been myself of late.

Now I'm not writing this to make excuses for myself or
leave the door open to any greater anti-testimony from a
senate of my peers but, please, welcome the Lethargic
Anarchists, who by their very nature are the bulk of my
acquaintances. The password to their hearts is the title of
their memoirs, written each day, in a fine debtor's hand.
Not disenfranchised, but accomplices — silent and stealthy
Alert, on a moment's notice, to avoid complex intimacy
when a simple yes will do.

They bear me no ill but concede me my illness. They hope
for repair yet carry no tools. We share a common trial:
Making strange heroes who leave post-its as referrals to our
character; a smattering of truth that does not adhere.

One Body

It's amusing the noise
the living make.

Listen the next time
a friend says he's done.
No more. All gone.
It isn't fair to Mary.

An airless silence. Then,
as if to sanitize the crime scene,
a broad exhale sweeps across extinction.
Those three, maybe four feet
serrating life and death.

They give you other options
but morphine's best.
One body making abrasive rasps
like the IRT brawling into Fulton,
clashing, blurring, fading to steam

Roswell

It was Roswell where we parted.

"I sell gum," I said.
She seemed surprised by that.

"I sell shoes," she said
as the air became submissive.

"I never opened Tuesday's door."

"Me either," she said, monochrome.

The whole conversation had lost its appeal,
I turned toward the alien crash.

Her Finery

Like soot upon her finery
the ash of my nature
alights. Under surveillance
our talk turns sour. Science,
sadism. The work of words.
We both know, my antagonist and I,
that someone's burying the bones.
That everyone shoots
from the same dirty needle
and populist men make war.

The Gnomist

A strange, sensational paragraph
inserts itself into my narrative,
chokes the captain's toupee to the floor.

The producers are watching closely
to see if I'll pack the house
w/congressmen, w/whores.

Courting the machine's mask,
a baleful, crying moon
reneges knowledge for desolation.
We all work for warring nations.

And that is how
those Mad Max movies
get started: The money tanks,
the food goes rotten, and
everyone walks in the same ugly boot.

Mongrel

An explosion
of packing peanuts ensures
I'll check Caucasian
on my donor form.

The blond patroness
licks the froth
off my imagination.

You never know
who lives next door
until you need

to plow their daughter.
Send their sons
to fight your wars

Sacrament

I got there early 'cos
that's what Dad would do.
Why keep the next guy waiting?
Felony always falls. It's a given.
No one is spared
the befuddled plots.

My deceptions, though many,
fall short of your legion.
Buddha's new coat
has many holes
and I have no thread.
No thimble. No wine.

a history of feminist driving

A century ago, a twenty-two year old
Hackensack mom, Alice Huyler Ramsey,
took off towards Poughkeepsie
in her thirty horse Maxwell DA
bound for post-quake Frisco.

Albany. Herkimer. Utica. In Auburn
she springs a Maxwell mechanic from jail
long enough to replace the coil.
In Ashtabula, a right turn
at the yellow house painted green
throws her off course
but that's hardly a thrill.

Nettie and Margaret, her tight ass in-laws
and sixteen year old Herminie, show no signs
of the *"endangered feminine psyche"*
the men in medicine swore occurred
when women drove over twenty. So imagine
how Vassar tapped the alumni for this gritty show:
Graduate fords Montezuma's Swamp
carrying water for the radiator
in cut glass toiletries. Scrounges canned tomatoes
from a general store. Defies a plank bridge
across Twain's river. Gets bedbugs in Wyoming.
A posse in Ogallala suspects her of murder.
A prairie dog hole outside Sioux City
blows the front axle. She braids wire
around steel
for repair.

Fifty-nine days and eleven flat tires later
the *"pretty women motorists"*
ride Market Street into history.
She returns to New Jersey by train.
The trackless land is never the same.

All the Lawns Are Perfect

If you can't convince them, confuse them
I deduced once while pissing,
so here goes: It's beautiful out there
you dumb motherfuckers. The trees are green.
The air is clean. We all share the cloud
w/o bicker. We live in grand culture
w/o GMOs. We stand indivisible.
w/Liberty. And Justice. For all.

wrinkled, blue

Blondie's tits doomed
Dagwood's estate.
But Dag didn't care
just give him the girl.

Now Cookie's a Coulter and Alexander
builds weapons he finds online. Herb pins his nipples.
Elmo's doing time for fire bombing
Cora's Spa of Happy Endings,
where Tootsie worked the trampoline
for Beasley's thug militia. And her tits don't sag
like fallen stars. Like his nuts, wrinkled, blue.

The Blonde w/Blue Shoes

In the mountains above other mountains
I'm playing footsie w/The Green Widow
at a table in a lobby full of women where baseball
and murder never end well. Back in the day before every
fucker was suspect, the vodka wouldn't cloud my judgment.
But here I am w/some backwater hottie w/bullets in her hair
and secrets in her jewelry no loupe can find. But that's how
it is in these small mountain towns where the moon is
never full

Her trio nimble

w/skin as tight
as a snare drum
she drifts off point.

she's vulnerable to the scratch
and her liner notes are too hard
to read. Her coda
an hourless patch.
Her trio nimble
like glacial rock.

Bereft in green zone larder,
she needs a new bassist and I
need a drink. A confidante
to the melody, a cohort
to the groove.

Wounded Cassandra

Wounded Cassandra
was a fictive kid
Who never escaped
her absolutes.

Everyone's passion
but no one's bargain,
Her clamorous vigor
kept men at war.

She breeds her own humor
by passing out matches.
Hordes her water
far from town.

Hitler's Florist

Hitler's Florist came and went
as he pleased. Twenty-four seven. A busy man
bearing lilies to Berlin. Mixed bouquets
to circus girls. He was fond of the circus, after-all.

Hitler's Florist was a family man
who dressed his children for Adolf's parades.
Added color to his paintings
of flowers, dogs, and girls.

Color Code

I've outsourced my brain
to square, colored paper.

Yellow immediate.
Blue tomorrow.
Gray indefinite
back burner stuff.

Pink for her.
An orange alarm.
Lavender missions
cling to the fridge.

Maggie's Piano

Air colored blocks of prime time
melt the cyanide in my glass.

Civil War chic is hot again.
Hedge fund angels hand me cash.

Maggie's piano has no song.
Piss poor authors
pen piss poor prose.

No one respects
the hometown prophet.
Not even the girls
who liked him once.

They twitter and yield
to his aberrant longings.
Volunteer time
at his retreat.

Cocktail murmurs scour the bones.
The last injunction:
shop while you can.

The roar of colonels
demands men die.

Pacific Trash Vortex

When I first discovered
the Pacific Trash Vortex,

Twice the size of Texas
and currently on the move

I thought, "Star Trek, Star Date 4202.9"
as the Doomsday Machine

ate every planet in sight
And it blew my mind!

How do we dispose
of so much shit

That it's mutating at horse latitude,
migrating tenfold every ten years?

Tofu tubs trapped
in tropical gyres,

Bottle caps
choking seabirds.

Nurdles in the food chain.
Mermaid tears

eaten by plankton,
eaten by fish.

Eaten by our voracity.
Passed on by our lust.

My Meeting w/Vonnegut

There's an extremely Jewish guy
barking parking directions
from the fire tower
Where I'm trying to envision
the land at peace
But can't 'cos I'm feelin' like
I'm either gonna push this guy off
the sixteen-hundred feet
or jump the expanse
and park the car myself.

"You sow a sad intelligence,"
Vonnegut said, stepping from the rubble
as only Kurt could: disheveled, all-knowing,
trying to bum an unfiltered
from a crowd of gerrymandered breeders
and the children they break.

"Here we are, trapped in the amber
of the moment," he said calmly,
pulling up his collar
against the mountain wind.

Purgatory Road

What do I hear, Walt Whitman
 But the drawl of morning traffic
 Along Purgatory Road.

Written in shit-finger,
the shareholder notes
drop from the fuller's hand,
as the pointillist dream
bleeds to form the boards between the sky.

In the parable I clamber Iron Mountain,
set the central bank ablaze.
Shit in the milk of this blood money.

In stone garden triage,
where I have yet to exhibit
 My mother's green thumb,
Zealots preen. Drop bombs.
Applaud their use of gravity.

In language too legal for truth
I edit the Bible slovenly.
Its veterans amassing
on dollies and gin.
A sad citizenry
fights without manner.
Frames for Pharoah
His blueprint. His waterless canals.

What I hear, Walt Whitman
I see ten times worse:
Where once beyond mountains
More mountains,
Now just a note –
Pull trigger.

Bio Hazard

If I manage
to get off this train
w/o diphtheria,
or consumption,
or some bio hazard
eating my innards
I'll recall this day fondly.

All on board coughing,
sneezing, hacking up
some germ from deep inside.
Some viral intruder
attaching itself
to my cold dime and dollar.

Raising a family on my liver.
Riding my tri-glycerides
slowly to my brain
and the net of nerves
that wraps my fingers
around my pen.

If it really takes root,
God knows.
I might write weirder than this.
A lyrical fist-fight of
fraught and humor.

If I get off this train
with any pulse at all
I'll stop by church tomorrow.
Pray for those sicker than I
only trying to get home.

Plum Colored V-Neck

I never knew
a plum colored V-Neck
could be a traffic hazard,
But that's my story
and I'm stuck with it.

Stray went my eye
as she walked by,
and we all know
how shit happens.

Eight car urban pile up
like mastodons in heat.

The peasant top
gave me tragic pause.
But at least I dodged
that group of nuns,
And that woman, with her shih-tzu
I missed her!
And the kid chasing dreams
in-between parked cars?
I missed him and Rabbi Klezmer!

But her plum-colored V-neck
broke my attention,
And now, your honor
if I may proceed . . .

Citizen's Arrest

I have never borne bullshit well
but today I've zero tolerance.

Bullshit is a quality of life crime
and I'm having you arrested!
C'mon, let's go!
Come quietly or I'll break your legs.
I've had enough of your peculiar logic
that frees you from responsibility
and dumps it on my front lawn!
I've had enough of your crab-assing discourse
About how mommy didn't make
Cherry jello on that morning thirty years ago
and *Homeland*'s on in five
and your clothes don't fit and
your husband's a twit and
your father's tweed knit
was a hit at the party
and your wife keeps IT from you
while soliciting IT from the rest of us!

Now I'm not Calvinistic
but you've got some time to serve.
Always unburdening yourself
by using the latest technology
as if these things were invented
To carry your old story,
your sloppy sagas of dissolution
and demise.

Well
Fuck you!
You're under arrest
and the judge is my brother

Erstwhile

Erstwhile is a funny town
where widows spread wide
for new recruits.

Erstwhile has very nice people
w/very good aim. Who drop defectors
from three hundred yards.

Erstwhile creeps east.
Heavily armed and opiated
by a spiteful god.

Erstwhile, in honorable times,
would have been
a center for reason

Instead of the shooting
we watch w/o tears.

The Girl and her Parachute

The girl and her parachute
were an enigma
from the moment
I picked her up.
Six miles from where
she planned to land.

Thanks for the ride, she said,
her parachute strangely mute.
So unlike my mother-in-law
going rogue in Vegas.

But this isn't about
any mother-in-law
past or present.
This is about the girl
and her parachute.
Who could have landed on my car
if the westerlies were buoyant.

You go for the buzz
'cos everything else is bullshit,
she said. And I had to agree
as the sky opened over Awosting
and two clouds were eloping.

Bone Box

I was the son of two Greek Cynics
w/a two day jump on the right wing,
rolling in on Picasso's horse
w/a burning need to pee.

I'd been holding it in since Rome and
here I was in Albuquerque, of all the unblessed places,
when a midlife couple from Elsewhere
hands me a map like I'm
defending cartography
from an 8.8 in downtown Broken Arrow.

A few years back, Dylan-esque strophs like these
wouldn't faze me. I'd double Paschal's wager
and go about my day
as impressionistic as possible
but the rebel latrines are disappearing
here in pistol-packin' America and to hell
w/that Graham Nash song. This is fuckin' war!

Closing

That ringing in my head
is not existential.
It's my super melodrama
early detection kit.

There's a hive of self-pity here
I know it. I can see it
with my night watch goggles

How sorry you feel
for feeling like you do,
When all I'm trying to do
is make a living
Selling words and theory,
Arguing a premise
based solely on my perception
and your consumption of it.

I'd like to thank you all
for coming tonight.
I'm sure you had other
plots to pursue
more meaningful, less stressful
on your constitution
than my irrevocable blather

But thanks for coming,
It would have been difficult
staying awake without you.

Acknowledgements

10th & Brutal – *WayMark #4, Summer 2015*

4,000 - *Relief Journal: An Expression of Christian Thought, 2008*
Purgatory Road, (Pudding House Press, 2010)

Adrift – *Eve's Venom (Post Traumatic Press, 2014)*

Ballad of Cigarette Monty (rw*) – Chronogram, Oct 2015   w/Will Nixon*

Bio Hazard – *Misfit, Spring 2013   Write Room, 2013*

Citizen's Arrest - *Compass Rose, 2009*

Clearing House - *Purgatory Road, (Pudding House Press, 2010)*

Couldn't I – *Long Island Quarterly, 2008*
Howland Cultural Center Playbill, 2008-2009
Purgatory Road, (Pudding House Press, 2010)

East 138 - *The Baltimore Review, Spring 2005*
Purgatory Road, (Pudding House Press, 2010)

Guest List - *Purgatory Road, (Pudding House Press, 2010)*

Half Shitty Days – *HeavenBone, 2009*

Her Finery - *Waymark Voices of the Valley # 3, January 2015*

High Diver – *Waymark Voices of the Valley # 3, January 2015*

Hitler's Florist (1st version) – *Krackers, Kids Like Us Press, 2015*

irony – *Waymark, Voices of The Valley, January 2015*
Calliope, 2015

It Was a Nice Day – *Penny Ante Feud #10, 2012*
Petrichor Review, 2013

Mongrel – *Gargoyle Magazine, 2009*
Earth's Daughters # 74, Spring 2009
Purgatory Road, (Pudding House Press, 2010)

My Inner Mexican – *Chronogram, February 2011*

My Meeting w/Vonnegut – *Negative Suck, 2014*
Forge 8.1 Summer 2014
Eve's Venom (Post Traumatic Press, 2014)

One Body – *Home Plant News, March 2015*

Our Holy Songs – *CAPS Anthology 2015   w/Will Nixon*

Pacific Trash Vortex – *South Carolina Review, 2010*
Pank, January 2010   Written River, 2013
Purgatory Road, (Pudding House Press, 2010)

Pale Diaspora – *The South Carolina Review, 2006*
Purgatory Road, (Pudding House Press, 2010)

Purgatory Road – *Purgatory Road, (Pudding House Press, 2010)*

Red Knots - *Written River, 2013*
Purgatory Road, (Pudding House Press, 2010)

Runner-up - *Eve's Venom, (Post Traumatic Press, 2014)*

Screaming Jay Hawkins and Me in Our Prime –
Panolopyzine, 2016

Sunny Lots – *Home Plant News, March 2015*

Tell Them, My Love – *Comstock Review, fall 2005   Riversedge, 2007*
Dyed In The Wool: Hudson Valley Anthology (Vivisphere,2000)
Purgatory Road, (Pudding House Press, 2010)

The Girl and Her Parachute – *Main Street Rag, 2014*
Eve's Venom (Post Traumatic Press, 2014)

The Gnomist – *Calliope, 2015*

The Old Shithouse - *Gihon River Review, 2008*

this vast engine – *Mad Hatter, Summer 2014   Calliope, 2015*

Weak Reeds – *Kracks, Kids Like Us Press, 2015*

Wounded Cassandra - *Literary Juice, 2012*

Mikes' poems and music criticism have appeared and/or are forthcoming in hundreds of magazines but have yet to generate any reportable income. Second chapbook, *Eve's Venom* (Post Traumatic Press, 2014) *Purgatory Road* (Pudding House Press, 2010) Anthologies: *WaterWrites* & *Riverine* (Codhill Press, 2009, 2007) *Will Work For Peace* (Zeropanik, 1999). VP, Calling All Poets in Beacon, NY. Producer of CAPSCASTS, recordings from CAPS, available at www.callingallpoets.net etc. Music features, interviews, & CD reviews appear in *Elmore Magazine* & the *Van Wyck Gazette*.

www.mikejurkovic.com

Special thanks to Hayden Wayne & Glenn Werner in making this book a reality.

He loves Emily most of all

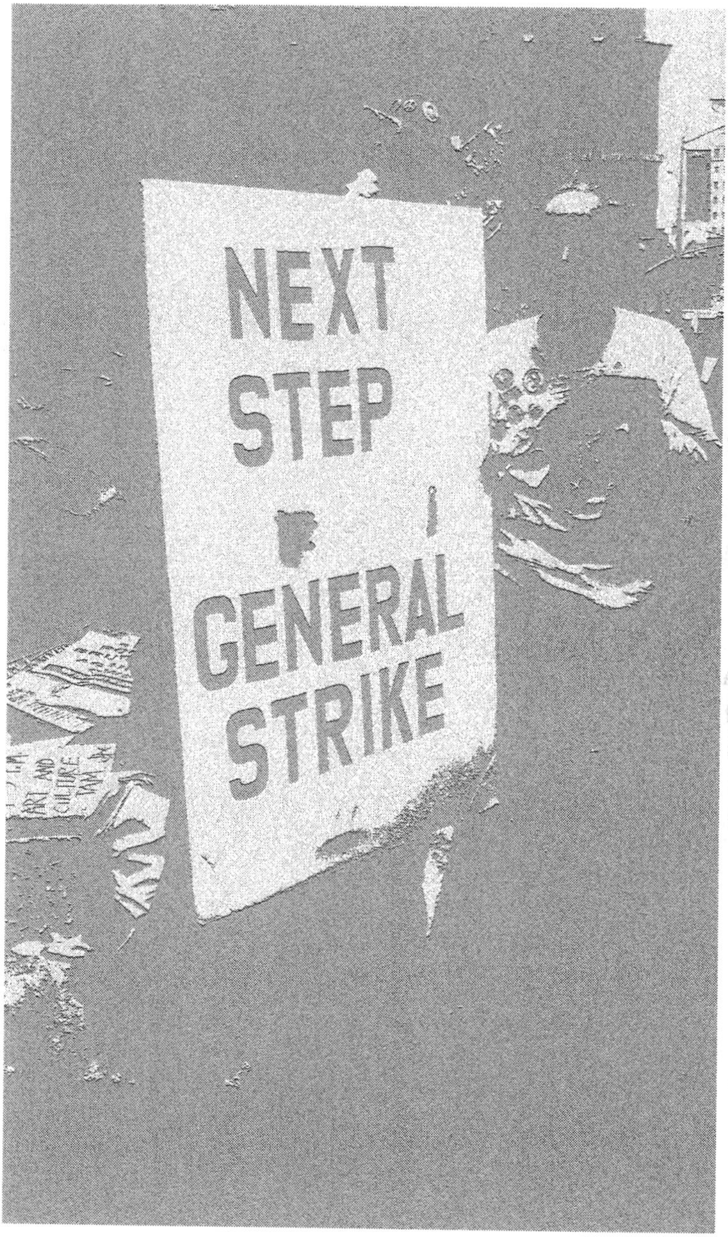
NEXT
STEP
GENERAL
STRIKE

Made in the USA
Charleston, SC
10 May 2016